D1613711

SandCastle

What Should I Eat?

Vegetables Are Vital

Amanda Rondeau

Consulting Editor
Monica Marx, M.A./Reading Specialist

Published by SandCastle™, an imprint of ABDO Publishing Company, 4940 Viking Drive, Edina, Minnesota 55435.

Printed in the United States.

Credits
Edited by: Pam Price
Curriculum Coordinator: Nancy Tuminelly
Cover and Interior Design and Production: Mighty Media
Photo Credits: Comstock, Corbis Images, Eyewire Images, ImageState, PhotoDisc

Library of Congress Cataloging-in-Publication Data

Rondeau, Amanda, 1974-
    Vegetables are vital / Amanda Rondeau.
      p. cm. -- (What should I eat?)
    Summary: A simple introduction to the vegetables group of foods and why vegetables are important for us to eat.
    ISBN 1-57765-835-3
      1. Vegetables--Juvenile literature. 2. Nutrition--Juvenile literature. [1. Vegetables. 2. Nutrition.] I. Title.

TX557 .R563 2002
641.3'5--dc21

                                                                          2002018361

SandCastle™ books are created by a professional team of educators, reading specialists, and content developers around five essential components that include phonemic awareness, phonics, vocabulary, text comprehension, and fluency. All books are written, reviewed, and leveled for guided reading, early intervention reading, and Accelerated Reader® programs and designed for use in shared, guided, and independent reading and writing activities to support a balanced approach to literacy instruction.

Let Us Know

After reading the book, SandCastle would like you to tell us your stories about reading. What is your favorite page? Was there something hard that you needed help with? Share the ups and downs of learning to read. We want to hear from you! To get posted on the ABDO Publishing Company Web site, send us email at:

sandcastle@abdopub.com

SandCastle Level: Transitional

What is the
vegetable group?

Fats & Sweets

Eat LESS

MILK Group
2-3
servings

PROTEIN Group
2-3
servings

VEGETABLE Group
3-5
servings

PEANUT BUTTER

TUNA

FRUIT JUICE

FRUIT Group
2-4
servings

GRAIN Group **6-11** servings

*For suggested serving sizes, see page 22.

This is the food pyramid.

There are 6 food groups in the pyramid.

The food pyramid helps us know how to eat right.

Eating right helps us stay healthy.

The vegetable group is part of the food pyramid.

We should eat 3 to 5 servings from the vegetable group every day.

Vegetables are good for our bodies.

There are many kinds of foods in the vegetable group.

Vegetables give us many vitamins that we need.

Vegetables make our bodies strong.

Did you know carrots
are a vegetable?

Carrots are orange and
give us a lot of Vitamin A.

Carrots are a great snack!

Did you know potatoes are a vegetable?

People in America eat a lot of potatoes.

Some people like baked potatoes and some like mashed potatoes.

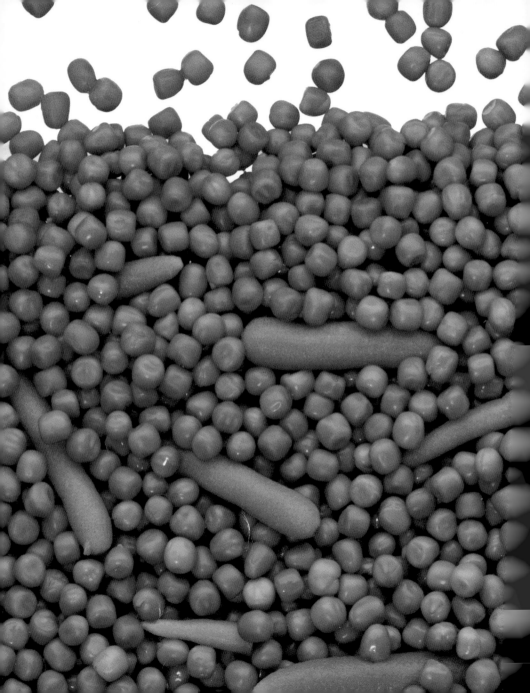

Did you know peas are a vegetable?

Peas are green and grow in pods on a vine.

Sometimes we eat peas and carrots together.

Did you know corn is a vegetable?

Corn can be yellow, blue, or white.

We eat mostly yellow corn.

Some people like to eat corn on the cob.

Can you think of other foods in the vegetable group?

What is your favorite food in the vegetable group?

Index

What Counts As a Serving?

Vegetable		
1 cup of raw leafy vegetables	½ cup of other vegetables, cooked or chopped raw	¾ cup of vegetable juice

 22

Glossary

baked   cooked in an oven

body   all the parts that make people or animals

favorite   the thing you like best

orange   a color made from red and yellow. Also a citrus fruit

pod   in some plants, the long part that seeds grow inside of

serving   a single portion of food

strong   powerful

vitamin   a substance that we need for good health, found naturally in plants and meats

About SandCastle™

A professional team of educators, reading specialists, and content developers created the SandCastle™ series to support young readers as they develop reading skills and strategies and increase their general knowledge. The SandCastle™ series has four levels that correspond to early literacy development in young children. The levels are provided to help teachers and parents select the appropriate books for young readers.

Emerging Readers
(no flags)

Beginning Readers
(1 flag)

Transitional Readers
(2 flags)

Fluent Readers
(3 flags)

These levels are meant only as a guide. All levels are subject to change.

To see a complete list of SandCastle™ books and other nonfiction titles from ABDO Publishing Company, visit **www.abdopub.com** or contact us at:

4940 Viking Drive, Edina, Minnesota 55435 • 1-800-800-1312 • fax: 1-952-831-1632